Copyright © [2018] by [Michael B. Schoettle]
All rights 979 - 8636653202
ISBN: -9798518089938.

The subtitle of this book was inspired by the poem,
THE ROAD NOT TAKEN, by Robert Frost.
.The last three lines are:
> "Two roads diverged in some wood, and I—
> I took the one less traveled by,
> And that has made all the difference."

Introduction

How do you feel about the work you are doing and the organization where you are working? Are you bored and doing an OK job? Are you looking for a new job? If so, view this moment as an opportunity. Be curious and optimistic.

You are not alone. Others have been in your situation. They have felt disappointed, scared, ambitious, motivated, and hopeful. Many have come out in more appropriate and fulfilling situations. You can too.

I have worked for many different organizations for over fifty-five years. When working in one with different values than mine, I did my job and went along with the flow, and not much happened. When I was in tune with the values where I worked, I was energized, accomplished more, and progressed. I have written this book to share what I have learned to help you progress in your career.

The most important part of a job search, especially involving a career change, is to develop an in-depth understanding of your values. They are at the core of who you are and come into play in everything you do. Values are more complex and nuanced than they appear. Having a meaningful understanding of yours is critical to identifying, joining, and working in an organization that is right for you.

The book is divided into four sections, one for each stage of making a career change. The chapters are about specific steps to accomplish each stage with ideas, stories, and recommended actions. Space is provided at the end of each chapter for notes.

Section I - Step 1: MOST IMPORTANT
        Develop a good understanding of your values, competencies, and what work is right for you.

Section II - Step 2
>Network with people you respect and share values to get their ideas and referrals.

Section III – Step 3
>Interview employers to see how you would feel about working with them and what you would be doing.

Section IV - Get closure on a job that is right for you and start well with your new employer.

In reading this book, first look at the table of contents and thumb through the book to get a feel for what is in it. Give the first section a thoughtful read and do the Recommended Actions, for they form the foundation for whatever you do. Then, proceed with the chapters that make sense for you, based on where you are in your search. *The sooner you start, the better off you will be.*

Dedication

This book is dedicated to Dr. John Schlosser, who was a kind and thoughtful man. He was instrumental in my joining the executive search firm, Heidrick & Struggles, and mentored me during my first few years there. Working at Heidrick & Struggles with Dr. Schlosser's guidance changed my life.

Acknowledgments

Many have helped me write this book. I especially appreciate the contributions of the following people:

Bill Lindsey and **Rich Stafford,** who headed the EMBA program at Loyola Marymount University while I taught there. Both repeatedly encouraged me to write this book. **Candy Deemer,** my partner for 12 years at LMU, where we developed many of the ideas in this book, had great suggestions. **Kevin Commins**, a professional editor, edited an early draft. **Bill White,** who wrote <u>From Day One</u>, a book for young people starting out in their first job, read my first draft carefully and had helpful insights. **Joann Maciejewsky**, an independent executive search consultant, identified appropriate Internet and job search websites. **Jacques de Spoelberch**, a long-time friend and independent literary agent, had some useful suggestions. **Paul Keye** helped me by challenging my thinking. **Lee Ault** and **Michael Zellen** both recommended changes that I adopted. **Mayumi Shimose Poe,** a professional editor, made many substantive edits that brought more clarity to the ideas expressed. **Ryan Delane,** a website designer, was very helpful in many ways. My son, **Will**, had great ideas and contributed a lot. He helped design the cover, and he read and edited many drafts. My other son, **Tim,** gave the book a careful read and produced thoughtful insights. My wife, **Marcia**, reviewed the book throughout the process and made many useful edits.

Table of Contents

		Page
Introduction		3
Dedication		5
Acknowledgment		7
Section I	**Who You Are**	12
Chapter 1	**Your Values** Core Values Other Values Culture	13
Chapter 2	**How You Process Information** Reader or Listener Personality Type	22
Chapter 3	**Your Capabilities** Skills and Competencies Strength Finder	27
Chapter 4	**The Right Role for You** Work Preferences Core Business Interests Contribution Work Role	33

		Page
Section II	**Your Search**	45

Chapter 5	**Stay or leave**	46
	Employment Status	
	Great Opportunity	

Chapter 6	**Your Search Plan**	50
	Your Resume	
	Elevator Pitch	
	Compensation	
	New Possibilities	

Chapter 7	**Your Network**	60
	List of Contacts	
	Setting Priorities	
	Meetings	

Chapter 8	**Other Search Approaches**	67
	Internet	
	Direct Approach	
	Search Firms	

Section III	**Interviewing**	74

Chapter 9	**Interview Preparation**	75
	Research the Organization	
	Prepare Questions	
	Prepare to Answer Questions	

Chapter 10	**The Classic Job Interview**	79
	Preparation	
	Pre-interview	
	Interview Phases	
	Post Interview	

		Page
Chapter 11	**Other Interview Situations** Types of Interviews Observations	85
Section IV	**Closure and New Beginning**	89
Chapter 12	**Compensation & References** Compensation References	90
Chapter 13	**Getting an Offer or Not** Good Offer Marginal Offer Unacceptable Offer No Offer	93
Chapter 14	**Joining the New Organization** New Boss Respect and Extra Effort Good Relationships Learning Though Experience	98
Epilogue		103
About the Author		105
Bibliography		106

Section I - Who You Are

Before searching for a new job, especially one involving a career choice, make sure that you have an in-depth understanding of who you are, especially your values. Then identify what you do best, what role is right for you, and what you want your contribution at work to be. By knowing yourself well, you will have a good understanding of what is important to you about where you work. You can then begin your search for an organization where you will feel good about the people there and do well.

Chapter 1 - Your Values

Your values are fundamental to who you are. They develop when you are young, and although they may evolve, they stay with you throughout your life.

Core Values

Core values form the guiding principles of our behavior. They come from our experiences with family, friends, and community. As adults, we develop our best relationships with people who have the same values as we do.

Having an in depth understanding of your Core Values is essential to knowing yourself. They remain with you as you age, although specific ones may become more-or-less important as your perspective changes. Core Values may appear common to most people, but the relative importance and meaning for each person will differ.

When values conflict, one will take precedence over another. For instance, if someone with limited capability whom you care about does something only satisfactorily, you might accept it. Yet, you would not accept this performance from a different person. In this example, Caring topped Excellence.

To develop an understanding of your Core Values, look at each of the values listed below and ask yourself what each means to you. Think of examples in your own life. For instance, what does Fairness mean to you? In our society, the understanding of Fairness has evolved in recent years. One person might say, "Everyone has the opportunity to do that, so that is fair." Another might say, "Some people are disadvantaged due to their birth and that is not fair."

Honesty: truth telling and being open

Integrity: acting consistently with one's principles

Promise keeping: fulfilling the spirit of commitment

Fidelity: being faithful and loyal

Fairness: treating people justly

Caring: having compassion and being kind

Respect: appreciating the human dignity of others

Citizenship: being a responsible member of the community

Excellence: performing at the highest level

Accountability: taking responsibility

Social consciousness: focusing on the greater good

What we think and say are our values and may not be what they really are. Since our actions reflect our values, to know yours, you need to consider your actions. Look at past decisions, especially important ones such as job changes. Ask yourself, "What were the values that influenced me to make those decisions? How did I feel afterwards?"

You may think that money, power, and position are values. While they might appear to be values, they are not. Ask yourself, "Why is making or having money important to me?" On the one hand, your answer could reflect your values, such as the desire to support your family or to have personal freedom. On the other hand, focusing on making money might reflect something less noble.

One way to learn about your values is by considering your relationships with your family, friends, and colleagues at work. With whom do you have the closest relationships? What are the values you have in common with them?

John Kroger is an example of someone who made his values the basis of his career choices. *After graduating from law school, he wanted to help society, always believe in what he was doing, and never compromise his values. He decided to join the United States Attorney's office as an Assistant U.S. Attorney for the Southern District of New York.*

Almost immediately, Kroger became deeply involved in an important case against the Mafia. When the head prosecutor could no longer work on the case, Kroger took the lead. In an intense and highly publicized battle, he won the case. This success immediately resulted in his becoming one of the leaders of the Southern District of New York office prosecuting the Mafia and major drug kingpins.

Kroger was successful. While he enjoyed winning, he became disenchanted. To prosecute a Mafia leader, a U.S. Attorney typically obtains evidence against a lower-level person in the organization and then gives that person the option of providing evidence against his bosses and receiving a reduced sentence. Kroger did this, but in so doing, he placed informers in precarious positions. Some were identified by the mob and murdered. Furthermore, after a mob leader was sent to jail, someone else would take over.

Kroger found himself worrying about the ethics of manipulating lower-level mobsters and getting some of them killed. Drugs were still being pushed. This did not sit well with him, and he decided to quit. Instead of becoming a highly paid defense attorney, which is the usual track for a successful U.S. Attorney, Kroger joined the University of Oregon as a professor of law.

Kroger was there only a short time when a former colleague at the Southern District of New York U.S. Attorney's Office called and asked him to join the team prosecuting the Enron financial fraud case in Texas. At that time, Enron was viewed as at the highest level of crime in corporate America. Kroger agreed and immediately became a part of the investigation into Enron's chief financial officer, Andrew Fastow. The government team discovered that Fastow had illegally transferred funds under his wife's name. Even though she had no other involvement, this action put her in legal jeopardy. When the government team gave Fastow the opportunity to cooperate with them to keep his wife out of the case, Fastow cooperated.

Kroger did not like how he felt about this and saw it as no different than what he had been doing against the mob. Consequently, he quit the government's Enron prosecuting team and returned to teaching law.

(Source: Kroger's book, <u>Convictions: A Prosecutor's Battles Against Mafia Killers, Drug Kingpins, and Enron Thieves</u>.)

Kroger's Core Value of wanting to do something that benefits society drove his career choices. How do your Core Values impact your career choices?

Other Values

Other values and considerations can become important when making work choices. Any career choice should include consideration of loved ones, community, and personal commitments. Your spouse's situation could affect where you live or how much time you are able to devote to your work. You could have involvements in your community or other interests that take up a lot of your time and are important to you.

One's personal situation can take on primary importance in a decision about work. For instance, some women who have young children want to leave work at a specific time, usually earlier than their peers. These women should work only for organizations that understand and honor these needs.

I know someone who grew up in a small city in Upstate New York. *He spent five years after college in various parts of the country but moved back to Upstate New York to be near his family and the community he loved. He recently changed jobs and only considered opportunities near the community where he lives.* His feelings about his family and community acted as values in his decision to work only in Upstate New York.

Culture

Another important consideration is culture. We all have a sense of our own culture. It influences how we relate to others, our values, outlook on life, and priorities. Where we work has a culture of its own, and it is important that we feel comfortable with it.

Understanding your own culture and that of where you want to work can help you make good job choices.

People's personal culture begins early in life and results from relationships with their family and the community in which they grew up. This includes the parent's social-economic status, behaviors, and attitudes about many aspects of their lives. Their community's norms, customs, and ethnicity also affect their values.

Think about your life. Yes, you have changed, and you have moved on from the culture in which you were raised. Some vestiges of it remain with you today. Can you think of any? There could be many, but you may not be aware of them.

Other important considerations about an organization's culture are its pace, interplay of its values, decision-making processes, and treatment of employees or members. These affect how an organization relates to the world and the dynamics of its operations.

Organizations in the same fields can have different cultures. For instance, an organization that manages wealthy people's money could have a thoughtful, long-term approach with responsibility and continuity being important. People in this organization will be measured, courteous, and collaborative. Yet another financial organization that has high risk/high returns as its objective could emphasize risk taking and rapid-paced, short-term, focused decision making. Here the people might be abrupt, profane, and competitive. Every organization is unique.

I know of a U. S. Coast Guard Officer whose ship was in port when he was transferred to an identical ship in the same harbor. *He walked across the dock and boarded his new ship. He found it to be squared away, with sailors who did their assignments well and treated each other with respect. He found a refreshing contrast to the ship he had just left. Also, the new ship performed at a higher level. The difference? The skipper of the new ship had high standards and respect for others that permeated the ship's crew.*

Even within the same parent organization, individual operating units can have different cultures.

Values and culture are often the most important considerations in decisions about work choices. Consider Sally's story. *The daughter of an Army officer, she lived in Europe while growing up and visited many art museums while she was there. In college, she studied business administration and minored in art history. After graduation, she went to work for a high-end retailer that was expanding. She liked the fact that the company had a lot of young, high-spirited people with an optimistic, energetic culture.*

Sally did well and over time was promoted. After a few years, she was transferred to the London office to help manage the expansion of the business in Europe. She led a team that interviewed, hired, and trained hundreds of bright young people for new stores. These were exciting times for Sally.

Three years later, Sally returned to the United States and found a much different culture in the retailer's U.S. operations. The company had lost its mojo. Employees were more concerned about themselves than doing a good job. As a district manager, she dealt with poorly performing stores and people whom she had to fire. Meanwhile, the company began pressing her to implement policies that she thought were wrong. Sally no longer felt good about the culture of the company. She resigned.

Sally decided that she wanted to work in the art world and began to volunteer at local art galleries in her area. She applied for an intern position at a major art museum and was one of the few accepted. Soon after she became an intern, a job in Development became available. She applied, and she was selected.

For the next three years, Sally added new corporate donors and managed existing ones. Meanwhile she married and had a baby. Her husband was accepted into a U.S. Army program in which he would go to medical school in Washington D.C. with full pay as an Army officer. Sally resigned from the art museum and, with her husband and child, moved to Washington D.C. Once her child enters school, Sally plans to apply for a job in development at one of the major museums in Washington D.C. or wherever she is living.

Sally's move to a major museum put her in a different culture than the retail organization. The museum had a long-term outlook, with a focus on high-quality, and a pace that enabled Sally to develop her life outside of work. Now that Sally is married and has a child, her priorities have changed. They may change again when her child is older. One can expect Sally to contribute wherever she is.

It is important to have the same values as those with whom you work and to feel good about your employer's culture. When in this situation, you will be productive and do what is right for your colleagues. They, in turn, will want to help you. A win-win for all.

Recommended Actions

Identify your Core Values, especially the ones that are most important to you.
1. Consider your life decisions and identify what values of yours influenced each decision and how you felt about it at the time.
2. What are the values of your family members, friends, and others whom you respect?
3. Review the values listed in this chapter.
4. Identify the three or four Core Values that are most important to you.

Identify other value-like considerations.
1. Identify any major considerations or circumstances that you feel are important in deciding what you do and where you work.

Develop your thoughts about your personal culture.
1. Identify the culture of your parents and the community in which you grew up.
2. Determine what is now your personal culture.
3. Identify the culture of where you want to work.

Make a list of the values and important considerations relating to where you work next.
1. Include the most important Core Values, culture and other considerations you have identified.
2. Prioritize this list.

Notes

Notes

Chapter 2 - How You Process Information

Understanding how you process information and make decisions will help you get a good sense of what work you do best. Knowing this will also help you understand how others process information and make decisions.

Reader or Listener

Peter Drucker was a management consultant, educator, and author who made a major contribution to the philosophical and practical foundations of modern business management. He thought it was important for someone to understand how he/she gathers information and makes decisions. Drucker focused on the question, "Are you a reader or listener?" Most people never think about this. Knowing if you are a reader or listener can help you when gathering information, making decisions, and communicating with others.

Drucker pointed out that President Eisenhower, a former Army General, operated in a culture that had a clear chain of command and well-defined objectives. He would make decisions and then communicate them in writing according to the chain of command. He followed two presidents whose earlier careers were in politics and were used to dealing with competing points of view expressed verbally by an array of independent power sources. These presidents were less structured and communicated their thoughts verbally. Eisenhower had trouble dealing with old school politicians.

Another question Drucker asked is, "How do I learn?" Some people learn by first discussing a topic, then thinking about it. Others learn by organizing their thoughts, then discussing the matter. The same questions can be asked about how you make decisions. Knowing this can make you more effective in your decision making and understanding how others process do as well.

Source: *"Managing Oneself"* by Peter Drucker, Harvard Business Review, March/April 1999)

Have you ever thought about how you process information and make decisions? If not, you could start now by asking yourself and observing the people with whom you work and live.

I process by first mulling over an idea in my mind before I discuss it with others. One of my sons thinks things through by first discussing ideas with others. He articulates his thoughts and gets feedback to help him understand an idea better. Sometimes he will say that he is thinking of doing something that seems to me to be unreasonable even though he may not be thinking seriously about doing it. Years before I knew this about my son, it drove me 'nuts,' but not since I understood how he processes.

I know a couple who provide an interesting contrast. *If someone expresses a thought to the wife, she will think, "Why is this person saying that? What is he/she feeling? What is behind what is being said?" The husband will process the same expression of thought in a completely different manner and think: "What exactly is being said, and is that right? What is the context, and how does that fit with my understanding of the situation?"*

What about the people with whom you work? How do they process information? *I once worked for a manager who liked to gather his team together at the end of each day to discuss the day's events and anything else that came to mind. To some, these meetings seemed like a waste of time. However, this manager processed information by talking and listening, and these meetings helped him, and others keep abreast of what was going on in his department.*

Often there are significant differences between people in different functional areas. For instance, salespeople are often relationship oriented and will focus on peoples' thoughts and feelings. They want to develop a good rapport with their customers. Finance people are more analytical. They focus mostly on numbers and objective data, and they tend to be more reserved in their dealings.

Think about your boss. Does he/she like to receive written reports or talk to you and others in your group about what you are doing? Identifying how your boss processes would enable you to understand and interact with him/her better. How about your peers? How do they process information and make decisions?

Personality Type

The **Myers-Briggs Type Indicator®** (MBTI®) makes practical identifiers of the psychological types described by C. G. Jung, a Swiss psychiatrist and psychoanalyst who founded analytical psychology. The essence of Jung's theory is that much seemingly random variation in behavior is quite orderly and consistent due to basic differences in ways individuals perceive and make judgments.

The Myers-Briggs theory postulates that "Perception involves all the ways of becoming aware of things, people, happenings, or ideas. Judgement involves all the ways of coming to conclusions about what they perceived. If people differ in what they perceive and in how they reach conclusions, then it is only reasonable for them to differ correspondingly in their interests, reactions, preferences, and skills."

In developing the Myers-Briggs Type Indicator [instrument], Isabel Briggs Myers, and her mother, Katharine Briggs, sought to make the insights of Jung's theory accessible to individuals and groups. They focused on two related thought processes in the development and application of the MBTI instrument: addressing a situation and making a decision.

They developed four preference categories that result in the following identification and description of personality types:

Favorite world: Do you prefer to focus on the outer world (Extraversion [E]) or your own inner world (Introversion [I])?

Information: Do you prefer to focus on the basic information you take in (Sensing [S]), or do you interpret and add meaning (Intuition [N])?

Decisions: When making decisions, do you focus on evidence and logic (Thinking [T]), or do you focus on relationships with others and your feelings (Feeling [F])?

Structure: In dealing with the world, do you prefer to get things decided (Judging [J]), or do you prefer to stay open to new information and options (Perceiving [P])?

Your Personality Type: When you decide on your preference in each category, you have your own Personality Type, which can be expressed as a four letter code with each identified by a single letter and are combined to form 16 personality types. For example, INTJ's prefer (Introversion, Intuition, Thinking, Judging), and ESFP's (Extroversion, Sensing, Feeling, Perceiving).

Each personality type identifies the personal characteristics, interactions with others, preferences at work, and potential blind spots of the person. In summary, INTJ's "Have original minds and great drive for their own ideas and purposes," and ESFP's are "Spontaneous, Resourceful, and Outgoing."

(Source: "MBTI® Basics." The Myers & Briggs Foundation, **myersbriggs.org/my-bit-personality-type/mbti-basics** and excerpted with permission from the MBTI® Manual: *A Guide to the Development and Use of the Myers-Briggs Type Indicator*)

To get your Myers-Briggs preferences, go to the Myers-Briggs website, **www.myersbriggs.org**, or search the Internet for Myers-Briggs. There are several levels of determining your preferences. These include: answering a multiple-choice questionnaire and receiving a short report for a small fee, purchasing a more complete description of the different preferences, and purchasing a one-hour session with a counsellor.

Recommended Actions

Determine your focus and how you process what you hear when talking to others.

1. On what do you focus when someone tells you something? Do you think about what the person is feeling or his/her ideas?
2. How do you process new information?
    a. First developing your thoughts about something, then discussing it with others.
    b. First discussing something, then developing your thoughts.
3. How do your colleagues at work and your family focus and process information?

If you have not taken the Myers-Briggs Assessment, consider doing so now. Then think about what this tells you about yourself.

Notes

Chapter 3 - Your Capabilities

Understanding your capabilities and what you do not do well can help you choose work that will enable you to chart a more productive career path and withstand the inevitable setbacks.

Skills and Competencies

What are your skills and competencies?

> **Skill:** a one-dimensional ability that a person can do naturally. Some people can quickly grasp other people's feelings. Others may be able to compute numbers in their heads. These are skills. A skill can be improved by training and experience. Skills are frequently incorporated in someone's preferred way of processing and interacting with others.

> **Competency:** a multidimensional ability to combine skills with knowledge and experience to generate a desired outcome. For example, good leaders combine abilities in strategic thinking and assessing team members' capabilities with training and supervisory experience to lead effectively. Good managers in finance easily understand numbers and combine this with education and experience in finance to do their jobs well.

To identify your skills and competencies, look at your personal history in different stages of your life. Think of situations, especially ones that went well where you played an active part. Identify your role in these situations and your contribution to the outcome. Start by looking at the near past, including your current and most recent jobs, community involvements, and family activities. Consider your high school and college experiences. What were your successes?

What did you do to achieve them? Which did you enjoy the most? What do these experiences tell you about yourself?

What have you done that did not turn out well? Have you failed at anything? Most people have. That is OK. Failing often means that one has tried to do something without enough knowledge or experience. One can learn from this. Most successful people have failed at least once. Giving time and thought to what caused a failure is an excellent way of understanding what to do and what not to do in the future.

Do you see any pattern to your work history and life choices? What does this tell you about yourself? What skills and competencies do you have? Ask someone with whom you have worked and get that person's thoughts. The more specific the feedback, the better.

Think about the future. What skills and competencies would you like to incorporate in what you do next? Do you see opportunities that would require developing a competency where you have the basic skills but need more experience and training?

StrengthsFinder

If you feel onshore what are your competencies or want to confirm your thinking, you can go to **gallupstrengthscenter.com** and for a small fee take the StrengthsFinder assessment, which identifies your Top 5 "Signature Themes." The accompanying materials you receive will describe how each theme is incorporated in your thoughts, perceptions, and behaviors. These are designed to give insight into how you approach your world, the role you often take, and what you think is important. A more extensive StrengthsFinder report is also available for an additional fee. It provides a complete strengths profile that ranks thirty-four strengths.

The StrengthsFinder results will give you a different perspective than Myers-Briggs. Together, they can help you understand yourself better, identify competencies that you do not possess but would like to have, and explore competencies that may not have occurred to you.

Another way to gain perspective on your skills and competencies is to ask those who know you well what they see as your strengths. You could review your StrengthsFinder report with them and ask them to comment on it and ask if they have any other ideas or insights.

Candy Deemer, with whom I worked closely at Loyola Marymount University (LMU), has a background that shows the relationship between values, competencies, and culture at work. *Candy grew up in Southern California. In high school she was Editor-in-Chief of the school newspaper. At Northwestern she majored in journalism. When she took two classes in advertising, she became fascinated by how advertising combines graphics with text and appeals to people's emotions. She decided to study advertising further.*

While in graduate school, Candy saw that, though interested, she was only moderately good at the creative part of advertising. She was much better suited for the account executive role that involved managing the client relationship.

After getting her master's, Candy joined Needham Harper & Steers in Chicago as an Assistant Account Executive. The firm had a great culture. Both the account executives and the creative people were professionals and worked well together. Candy enjoyed her time there. However, after two years, Candy decided that she wanted to return to California.

Candy soon lined up a job with a small advertising firm in San Francisco. Once at the new firm, she learned that it had good account executives but a dull creative department. It was hierarchical in its managing processes, and people did not collaborate with each other. The head of the firm ignored the junior people.

Candy was at the firm about a year when she received a call from a friend who was working for Doyle Dane Burbank (DDB) in Los Angeles. The friend asked Candy if she was happy where she was. At first Candy demurred, then admitted that she hated it. The friend told Candy that DDB had a great office in Los Angeles and suggested that she come and meet the team. Candy did and soon joined DDB as an Account Executive.

Candy did well at DDB, and over her years there, she was promoted several times and ended up as Co-Managing Director of the Los Angeles Office. While in that role, she hired a coach to work with her subordinates. Candy was impressed by the coach and hired the coach to help her understand herself better in both her professional and personal lives.

After considerable thought, Candy decided to leave DDB. Candy was promotable there, but the opportunities were all outside of Southern California. When she left, she wrote a book for women in business, Dancing on the Glass Ceiling, co-authored with her coach, Nancy Fredericks. It was well received, and for the next year the two of them gave lectures and programs for various organizations. Then Candy began co-managing a career planning course and coaching program for the EMBA's at LMU with me.

After about 12 years Candy decided to become a professional executive coach and completed a program for professionals in this field. She is now doing well as a coach and finds it to be interesting and personally rewarding.

In reviewing Candy's career choices, one can see that she was true to her values, competencies, and feelings about the culture and people where she worked. She did well and contributed wherever she was.

How do you feel about what you are doing? Are your values in tune with those of your colleagues? Are your skills and competencies incorporated in your work? Do different paths come to mind, and, if so, which one makes the most sense for you?

Recommended Actions

Identify your skills and competencies.
1. Review what you have learned about your skills and competencies.

2. What skills and competencies were in play in your recent and past accomplishments?
3. Identify your top two or three skills and competencies.

Focusing on competencies, determine:
1. To do well at the work you do or want to do, what competencies are needed?
2. Which of these competences do you already possess, and which do you need to obtain?
3. Identify the competencies you would most like to incorporate in your work.

If you took the StrengthsFinder course, determine how the strengths identified relate to your skills and competencies.

Notes

Notes

Chapter 4 - The Right Role for You

People can do their best if their role incorporates not only their values, skills, and competencies but also other aspects of who they are. These include their preferred work environment, business interests, and whom or what they want their work to benefit. Knowing this will help them choose a job that makes the most sense for them.

Work Preferences

People's work preferences reflect many aspects of who they are, both their rational and intuitive selves. Their energy and personality help determine their preferences and impact everything they do. Go over this list and choose one or the other of each of these trade-offs and see what your choices tell you about yourself.

- **Collaboration vs. Competition**
- **Teamwork vs. Individualism**
- **Process vs. Results**
- **High Risk vs. Low Risk**
- **Relationships vs. Results**
- **Creativity vs. Rationality**
- **Perfection vs. Production**
- **Idealism vs. Pragmatism**
- **Leading vs. Following**
- **Doing vs. Advising**
- **Privacy vs. Openness**
- **Unpredictable vs. Predictable**

You could learn more about your work preferences by considering which ones were in play when you made job choice decisions and your feelings once there. Do you see a pattern, and if so, what is it? How do you feel about the match up of your preferences with where you work now or recently worked? Ask yourself the same questions about your choices in school and activities outside of school.

Greg's job at a publishing company was to create, identify, and develop major events or initiatives that would bring visibility to the company. He was particularly good at the job, but the company was constantly reorganizing. Greg had to educate each new boss about what he was doing and get approval for his projects. Greg wanted more autonomy so he could move fast and take risks. Finally, Greg had enough and quit.

Greg then joined a major shopping center company to create and manage events to attract people to the company's centers. However, he soon realized that here too he had to get approval for everything he wanted to do and that the culture was slow moving and risk adverse.

When Greg received a call from a former boss who was running a small and aggressive company where special events were an important part of the business, Greg was intrigued and soon joined. Now he is happy to have more autonomy to develop and oversee special events with the freedom to do what he thinks makes the most sense.

Note that in both the publishing company and the shopping center organizations, their slow-moving decision-making and risk-averse processes bothered Greg. The problem was not a difference in values.

Core Business Interests

Another way of gaining greater understanding about what you most like to do at work is to identify what aspects of work feel best to you. Look at the following list of Core Business Interests and check the ones that might be of interest to you, even if you have not considered them before.

Core Business Interests

Category I: Application of Expertise

Application of Technology
Engineering
Computer programming
Production planning
Analyzing processes
Analyzing systems
Manufacturing

Quantitative Analysis
Analyzing investments
Analyzing market research
Forecasting
Building computer models
Creating schedules
Performing accounting tasks

Theory Development and Conceptual Thinking
Developing economic theories
Developing business models
Doing competitive analysis
Developing big-picture strategies

Designing processes
Teaching business theory

Creative Production

Designing new products
Marketing and advertising
Generating new ideas
Originating innovative ideas
Managing projects
Conducting public relations

Category II: Working with People

Counseling and Mentoring

Coaching, training, teaching
Developing Organizations
Managing human resources
Fostering mentoring-oriented management practices
Supporting and developing
Giving feedback or advice

Managing People and Relationships
Managing others
Directing
Supervising
Leading others

Motivating
Taking care of day to day operations

Category III: Control and Influence

Enterprise Control

Controlling business resources
Providing strategic direction

Influence through Language and Ideas
Negotiating
Deal-making

> Having decision-making authority   public relations
> Managing others   Persuading
> Holding ultimate responsibility   Designing advertising
>
> (Source: Harvard Business School Press, <u>Shaping Your Career</u>)

Most people's choices will show a pattern of favoring one column or the other within each category. After doing this for all three categories, ask yourself what your choices tell you. Do you see a pattern that reinforces your feelings about what you have been doing or one that gives you a new perspective about what you might do in the future?

Contribution

We all contribute to work in a variety of ways. No two people have the same feelings about the contribution that they want their work to make. For some, helping those with whom they work directly will be their focus. For others, assisting in the mission of the enterprise may be the most important. Still others will experience satisfaction simply with what they are doing.

In all cases people feel best about their work when it helps give their life meaning. If you ask successful elderly people what they feel best about in their work, they will invariably remember a contribution they made and their relationships with those they worked. Never will they rank having made a lot of money or having high status.

Several years ago, a woman was working in the product development department of a cosmetic and skin care company when a new department manager was appointed. He had a technical background but none in product development. This upset the woman, and she thought about quitting. However, when she spoke about this to her coach, the coach pointed out that this situation gave her an opportunity to help her boss and in doing so improve the productivity of her department.

The next week the woman met with her boss and offered to explain the programs underway and answer any questions he might have.

The boss accepted her offer. The two began working closely together as they reviewed the different programs. He appreciated the help, and the woman could see the impact she was having and felt better about working there. After a few months, the department manager promoted the woman. What are you doing to help your boss achieve what he/she feels is important?

Someone at any level in an organization can have a sense of the greater world in which they work. *Years ago, when President Kennedy was touring Cape Canaveral, he asked a janitor what he was doing. The janitor answered, "Mister President, I am helping put a man on the moon."*

Others may see themselves as part of an effort that stretches over generations. Business leaders, especially of privately owned companies, think in terms of having a multigenerational impact on their families and communities. Many scientists, researchers, and religious leaders have a similar perspective. I know a philosophy professor who is devoting himself to creating original ideas in analytical philosophy that he sees as being part of a thread of thought that traces back to Plato's Republic and will continue in the future.

Britton Chance was a scientist with a passion for pioneering and discovering new technologies. Most scientists who make an important discovery devote their careers to developing their discovery. Not this scientist. He made many discoveries during his long life. After his death, scientists from around the world, who had worked on his discoveries, gathered to honor his contributions and share their experiences.

What do you want to accomplish?
- Improve the performance of a team
- Deliver identifiable benefits to customers
- Contribute something you think is important

Who would you like to see benefit?
- The team or organization where you work
- Your customers, clients, or users

- An industry or professional field
- Someone or something else that you think is significant

Consider your past performance and contributions you have made in work, community, and family. What difference have you made? Who benefited? How did you feel about that? You may find that you have been thinking of your job as simply a source of money to take care of your family. That is honorable. However, what if you thought in terms of contributing to something that excited you? This would enable you to feel better and be more effect at whatever you do.

Work Role

The following is a description of roles at work and how they can change over a lifetime.

Evolution of One's Role at Work as One Ages

1. Beginning adult
    a. Finding his/her own way.
    b. Changing jobs several times looking for the right fit.
    c. Performing basic tasks.
2. Young adult
    a. Choosing a career direction and focusing on "making it."
    b. Working to progress in responsibilities.
    c. Getting established, becoming "own person."
    d. Working as a leader of a small group or a senior "doer."
3. Adult
    a. Having a management role at work.
    b. Working as a senior professional.
    c. Feeling a strong sense of self.
    d. Rebalancing work, family, and community activities.
4. Mature adult
    a. Performing at a senior level in an organization or on his/her own.

        b. Mentoring others and developing an organization.
    5. Older adult
        a. Working in strategic/advisory roles.
        b. Mentoring others.
        c. Spending more time with family/ friends.
        d. Returning to earlier interests

(Based mostly on Daniel J. Levinson's books, <u>Seasons of a Man's Life</u> and <u>Seasons of a Woman's Life</u>)

In what stage of adult development are you? Are you in a situation where your perspective is evolving, or has it remained the same for a while? Do you want to continue what you are doing, or do you want to change in some way? How does your work affect the rest of your life? How do you feel about this?

Mack worked for an information technology company in account management for key government customers. He decided he could do more. Mack volunteered to take over a sales training program. His boss appreciated Mack's taking on this responsibility. Mack gained experience and deepened his relationships with the salespeople. He then participated in a major, multilevel meeting with the company's primary customer. This went well. Mack's role at his company will continue to grow, largely because of his attitude of taking the initiative and offering to contribute wherever he can. What is your attitude about taking on responsibilities in new areas and helping others succeed?

People's roles and perspectives evolve over a lifetime. Others stay with one role for long periods and sometimes for most of their careers. Many mid-level managers and people in professional services are happy with the work they are doing and enjoy their independence. Almost any Naval Officer who has commanded a ship and then was promoted to a more senior level will tell you that the best job he/she ever had was captain of a ship. Someone who owns his or her own business and professionals in many fields will express similar feelings.

In the long run, it is most important that one's values are incorporated in one's work. Sometimes it takes a while for this to happen. Consider Arthur. His perspectives, roles, and goals evolved over his career. *He grew up in Brooklyn, New York, in a neighborhood where several neighborhood fathers worked for the city government. He respected these men for their contributions to the community and thought he might someday do the same. However, after a summer job with the government, he changed his mind. Yet, he kept the thought that he would someday like to do something to benefit others.*

After graduating from college and business school, Arthur joined a small brokerage firm in New York City and immediately did well. When the business was impacted by a major recession, many were laid off, and the president promoted Arthur to Sales Manager.

Later, Arthur joined a major financial company because he saw the potential to make more money. Arthur immediately found himself on a wild ride in the world of high finance, flying here and there, and doing very well. After a few years passed, Arthur's brother unexpectedly died. This jolted Arthur. He asked himself, "What am I doing?" He did not like the answer and decided to move out of New York City.

Arthur soon took a finance job in Los Angeles. Although the pace was not as frantic, the job was still about money. He was there for a short time when he joined the board of Chrysalis, a nonprofit with the mission of helping homeless people get jobs. He was impressed by the organization and its people. Not long after Arthur joined the board, the executive director left. Arthur took over the executive director role on a temporary basis at first and then permanently.

Arthur ran Chrysalis for several years, expanding its capabilities and increasing the number of people who got jobs through the organization's programs. He developed his abilities as a general manager and led this organization with great success. He valued the organization's mission, whereas he had little respect for what he had been doing before.

While in charge of Chrysalis, Arthur saw the need for professional managers to lead socially conscious, nonprofit organizations. He decided he could help fill this need and soon established a unit in a local university's MBA program. Its mission was to develop new strategies for solving social issues, such as poverty and homelessness. This provided a new path for students and faculty who want to use their business skills to benefit the world. The program has since grown into a substantial operation with a global reach.

Looking at Arthur's journey so far, it is clear he is a high achiever with multiple competencies. He wants to make things happen, and he has been successful in all his positions. With regards to his work choice priorities, he began with one idea, lost it for a while, and then regained it when he joined Chrysalis. Note that Arthur's roles evolved over time and that his values were the primary driver of his later job choices.

If you are puzzled about what work makes the most sense for you, keep a log. At the end of each workday, record what you most enjoyed about your work and why. Then identify what you did not like and why. After doing this for ten days, review and summarize what you recorded. Almost all who do this exercise find that it reveals something about themselves that they had not known. The same could be true for you.

If you were to write your obituary now, what would it say? How would you feel about it? What would you like your obituary to say? Redirect yourself to a new vision of what you want your life's story to be.

After doing the recommended actions for this chapter, you should have a good understanding of who you are, especially your values, competencies, and preferred role. In addition, you should have a good sense of your priorities for where you work next. If you feel that you have these, then proceed with the rest of the book. If not, review what you feel you need to know better and get a good understanding of that before proceeding.

Recommended Actions

Identify your top two or three Preferences.
1. Do you see a pattern in your preferences, and if so, what does it reveal?
2. What Work Preferences are incorporated in your work?
3. What Work Preferences do you want to be in your work?

Look at the Core Business Interests you checked and ask:
1. Is there a pattern? If so, what does it reveal?
2. How do these choices compare to your current job?
3. Do you see something of interest that you might want to do in the future?

Determine the contribution you want to make.
1. How does your work benefit your customers or clients?
   a. How do you feel about that?
   b. What change would make you feel better?
2. Who or what would you like your work to benefit?

Identify and assess your role at work.
1. Are you in the role that makes the most sense for you?
2. If not, determine what role would be best for you.
3. Do what you can to transition into that role.

If you are still puzzled about your preferred work role or your feelings about your current or previous job, consider doing the following exercise:
1. If you are currently working, at the end of each day:
   a. Record what you most enjoyed that day and why.
   b. Do the same for what you disliked doing.
2. Do this for 5-10 days, review your notes, and ask yourself what you learned about yourself.
3. If you are not working, ask the same questions about where you last worked and see what you learn.

List what you think is important about where you work and what you do.
- Core Values & Personal Commitments
- Competencies
- Work Preferences
- Preferred role
- Who or what you want your work to benefit
- Anything else that is relevant and important to you

In addition to this and the next page, consider using the space in the back of the book for your notes.

Notes

Notes

Section II - Your Search

If you are currently working and do not feel good about what you are doing, try to find an opportunity where you currently work. If nothing materializes, leaving is the right move. Then it becomes important to think about what to do next, update your resume, and develop a plan for your search.

Once you have decided to leave and have organized yourself, you can begin your search by meeting with experienced people whom you respect and who have a wider perspective. They could identify possibilities and refer you to others who could also help you. Additional ways to find opportunities include looking online and directly approaching organizations and search firms.

Chapter 5 - Stay or Leave

In the world of work, one must manage one's own journey. Employers, educators, consultants, and even family members will not have the same perspective as you have about where you work and what you do. Others can unknowingly be conflicted by their own interests and outlooks. Therefore, it is always best for you to develop and manage your own plans and actions related to work.

Many people looking for a career change have left their former employer because of actions taken by their employer. These people often have had to make a change with little or no preparation. It is better to take the initiative oneself and have time to plan and prepare for a job search.

Employment Status

If you are thinking of leaving where you work, you owe it to yourself to consider your options carefully. Ask yourself why you are not happy where you are now. If the problem is the work you are doing, there might be other opportunities available within the organization. If you have a good relationship with your boss, you could talk to him/her and see if a change in your role could be made. Otherwise, quietly look around to see if you identify an opportunity that would be a better fit. You might find something.

It can often be easier to move internally, especially if you have contributed to the organization and are well-regarded. However, if you are unhappy with your boss and you have been unable to identify another position of interest elsewhere in the organization, you have a problem. To get into a better situation, plan to leave.

If you keep working for your current employer while you search for another job, work hard, be conscientious, and make sure that your boss and others with whom you work feel good about what you are doing. Later, one of them may get a call from someone referencing you.

Leaving a job before securing a new one has advantages. You will have more time and freedom to find an opportunity that is right for you. Since your job search will not be confidential, you will be able to contact more people and get visibility for more opportunities. You might even be able to enlist the help and/or thoughts of colleagues where you worked.

If you are laid off or volunteer to be laid off, depending on your employer's benefit programs, you might be able to receive severance benefits. These could include unused vacation pay and/or continued salary and benefits for a period.

The U.S. Federal Government and most state governments provide resources and financial support for unemployed people. To find out what resources and support are available to you, call the U.S. Department of Labor Contact Center at 877 872-5627. Here you can learn about Federal Government policies and resources and the phone number of your state's unemployment office. Each state has its own set of benefits and procedures. Finding out what the Federal Government and your state offer could help you decide when to leave and provide resources after you have left.

If you have limited financial resources, consider looking for temporary work or a part-time job as well as unemployment benefits. You might even be able to get part-time work from your former employer. This will help you sustain yourself long enough to find the right place to work.

If you take the initiative to resign from your current employer, you will have more control of the process. When you notify your boss, be as positive as you can about it. You could say that you are leaving for personal reasons or because you want to go in another direction. Try to live in an orderly way.

In all cases, continue to do your best with your current employer while there. You will be acting responsibly and will feel good about yourself and your relationships with your colleagues.

Great Opportunity

Conducting a job search is a great way to get on a path that makes the most sense for you. Your search will probably uncover opportunities that you had not considered. This is your chance to explore and pursue something new.

In the process of conducting your search for a new job, you will meet and get to know people whom you respect. This will broaden and strengthen your network and could benefit you in unexpected ways in the future. Most successful people will tell you that this has happened to them.

While conducting your search, it is important to maintain a positive attitude with business contacts, friends, and especially family. If you see yourself as being on an adventure, they will too. The better you feel about yourself, the more effective you will be at everything you do.

Separate space at or near your residence can help you from being distracted. Using a separate landline or cell phone for your business would be helpful too.

Recommended Actions

Decide if you want to leave.
1. If you share the values and culture of your current employer, try to work something out.
2. Consider discussing your feelings with your boss.
3. Possibly meet with peers in other departments and see if there are any opportunities of interest.

If you decide to leave:
1. Continue to do your best work while you are there.
2. Strengthen your relationships with those you respect.
3. Find out your employer's and government's unemployment policies.
4. Leave in the best way you can.

Start your search well.
1. If short of funds, try to get part-time work.
2. Be positive, especially with your family.
3. Consider yourself to be embarking on a path of exploration and discovery.

Notes

Chapter 6 - Your Search Plan

Before you begin your search, you will need a resume that gives a good summary of who you are, your capabilities, and what you have accomplished to date. In addition, you will often be asked what you are looking to do. Be ready to respond with a short statement called an 'elevator pitch' that states what you have done and what you are looking to do.

Finding out the market value for someone with your experience and competencies can help you develop a realistic perspective. Begin identifying opportunities by contacting people you respect seeking their ideas and referrals.

Your Resume

Put a lot of effort into preparing your resume – it is your most important document. A well-done resume will give a good overview of your capabilities and achievements plus a broad sense of who you are.

Most people looking to hire someone have a specific job in mind and an idea of what qualifications a candidate should have. These days, qualifications are often expressed in terms of competencies. So, stating yours can help you get traction. If you have a specific job or sense of what you want to do next, include this in your resume.

Resumes are documents that need to present information about your work history, interests, and education. They must be in outline form and with as few words as possible and state facts and not descriptions of you, such as "great communicator" or "good leader." These lack credibility and do not come across well. Someone reading your resume will be most interested in what responsibilities you have had and what you have accomplished.

Resume Outline

YOUR NAME
(City, St, zip code, phone number, email address)

JOB OBJECTIVE and/or COMPETENCIES

EXPERIENCE

Company Name   (Start and end dates)
Address
   (Job title/ accomplishments)

   (Job title/ accomplishments)

Company Name   (Start and end dates)
Address
   (Job title/ accomplishments)
   (Job title/ accomplishments)

Company Name   (Start and end dates)
Address
   (Job title/ accomplishments)
   (Job title/ accomplishments)

EDUCATION

School name, Degree, Year degree obtained, and special awards/ accomplishments, if appropriate

OTHER

Interests, community services, achievements, and contributions

References available upon request

(You can find and download a resume template at the website - www.careerchange.guide.)

Job Objective and/or Competency Section will likely be the first place someone reading your resume will look. If you have a Job Objective on your resume, place it before Competencies. The Job Objective will be most effective if it states work you want to do and/or the contribution you want to make, not the role you want. For any job objective, your competencies and experience should be relevant.

Competencies should state your capabilities in a factual way without adjectives. The more competencies given, the less importance each will have. Too many gives the impression that the person lacks focus and has an inflated sense of what he/she can do well. Show two or three competencies at the most.

The Experience Section should be clear and concise in outline format. Someone reading it will expect to see the organizations where you worked, the city and state, the month and year you started and left, the positions you held, and your accomplishments. Several positions at the same organization strengthen your resume, especially if your responsibilities increased.

Show your accomplishments in phrase form with the accomplishment quantified, such as increased sales 25% or reduced expenses by $400,000. This gives them more credibility. If an accomplishment was as a member of a team, saying so will show you are a team player.

People put activities under each job thinking that this helps describe what they did. Yet, their accomplishments are much more important. Listing activities wastes space and detracts from accomplishments.

If you have already worked for 20 years or more, your recent jobs will be most interesting to someone reading your resume. You might combine earlier jobs in summary form with a few accomplishments. Having the experience section of your resume show a pattern of progress in responsibilities and/or gaining useful experience presents you in the best light.

The Education Section should show the institution(s) where you studied, degree(s) earned, and year(s) received. If your undergraduate degree or post-graduate studies relate to the type of work you look to do, your field of study could be important. However, if you have been out of school for a while, then only the fact that you have a degree is important in most cases. Employers are more interested in what you have accomplished and how well you relate to others.

People who do not include the graduation year usually do not want a potential employer to know their age or that they did not graduate. Someone reading a resume without this information will conclude that the year is not shown for one of these reasons and think the person for trying to hide something . This will cause a loss of trust in the person. Consequently, it is always better to show the years you were there.

The Other Section provides an opportunity for you to show who you are beyond work including your interests, activities, involvements, and accomplishments. Community involvement can show one's values and give a broader sense of the person. Being married with children shows responsibility and stability. A well-done Other Section can strengthen your resume.

The statement, "References available upon request" is normally at the bottom of a resume. Identifying references before beginning the search ahead of time will make sure they are in place when the need arises. When you first talk to your references, give each a good understanding of your decision to look for another job and what you have in mind. One of them might have useful ideas or referrals.

After you begin your search, give your references periodic updates on your progress. Call them only occasionally and send them email updates between calls to keep from taking too much of their time.

If you have multiple versions of your resume, keep a record of which one you have given each person to avoid problems in the future. You may want to revise your resume or you may want to create a specific resume for a specific opportunity. Good records can enable you to keep control and follow up properly with people you have contacted.

If you are looking for a position that requires creativity, you might display your resume in a unique format, such as adding a photograph of yourself and/or graphics. This could give your resume more visibility, complement your work history, and show your creativity. But do not overdo it.

Someone looking at your resume may see something that puzzles them and might ask you a question about it. To identify potential questions, you could ask someone you respect to take a critical look at your resume. Questions might cover:
- Why did you leave one employer and join the other.
- Gaps, either after college or between your jobs. Good interviewers will wonder why and probe.
- Mistakes you may have made. Mentioning these shows honesty, maturity, and potential for growth.

Once you have identified potential questions, decide how you will address each one, and be prepared to do so.

Elevator Pitch

Once you begin to let people know that you are looking for another job, you can expect that some will ask you "What's up?" An 'Elevator Pitch' can be helpful. It should briefly describe what you are looking to do, your work experience, organization you want to join, and the contribution you want to make. For example:

"I am looking for a financial management position at an early-stage company. I have ten years of experience in financial planning at mid-sized companies implementing new systems. I would like to put in systems to help a growing company sustain its momentum. Do you have any suggestions?"

"I am looking for a marketing management position with a consumer products company. I have 12 years of marketing experience for wine companies and an advertising agency. I want to join a consumer products company and help it launch new products and expand its customer base. Do you have any suggestions?"

If someone responds to your Elevator Pitch with questions, you could give a brief description of a contribution or two you made. You could also say what you are looking for in a new employer with a focus on what you can contribute. Be enthusiastic.

If you have left your former employer, you can expect people to ask you about the circumstances. Some will simply be curious. Potential employers will have a more serious interest. A short answer that is factual and expresses what you learned from the experience in a positive way would set a good tone.

Compensation

Compensation, except in a general sense, does not come up until late in the interviewing process. When it does, it is important to have a well thought out point of view. You could get some data for people with your experience from websites such as payscale.com, salary.com, and others. Checking with people you know who have insight into the market for someone with your experience could provide useful information. Your prior compensation is an important reference point.

New Possibilities

Companies and organizations that are growing or changing are more likely to need new employees. In today's world, many of them need to adjust to a dramatically changing environment and hire new employees.

Industries that have potential could be ones that relate to what you have been doing. If you have been in a products industry, consider working in a services firm that relates to the products or markets where you have been working. Review the Core Business Interests you identified in Chapter 4 might bring some ideas to mind.

To identify more options, take advantage of your freedom to explore any field of interest. Exciting opportunities can come from unexpected sources. Explore areas that you discover as the result of random meetings. If you want to move into an unrelated area, this is your chance. There are more opportunities out there than you think. Choosing the right one could change your life.

An effective way for you to learn about possible opportunities is to meet with people who have the knowledge and perspective to provide helpful insights. Most people, especially older and successful people, are happy to share their thoughts with someone who is trying to decide what they want to do next. Some of your peers could be helpful too.

Everyone feels honored when someone shows interest in learning his/her perspective. Being inquisitive and respectful sets the right tone. When you contact and meet people, express interest in them, their experience, and their thoughts.

People who refer you to job opportunities or others who can help you are called 'sources.' Their referrals are a great way to find opportunities. If you connect well with a source and the source suggests you talk to someone else, a potential employer or another source, you will connect well with that person too.

Your primary objective in meetings at the beginning of your search is to gather information about opportunities in areas that would be of interest to you. When meeting with someone, begin with a short overview of your work experience and your thoughts about what you think you want to do. This could include your competencies and what is important to you about where you work next. Then focus on the other person's experiences and perspectives, probing anything of interest to you and letting him/her know that you would appreciate recommendations he/she might have.

To strengthen your relationship with these people, look for ways to reciprocate, especially those with whom you would want to develop a long-term relationship. In all cases, follow up your meeting with a note thanking each person for his or her time and thoughts. This is always appreciated. For most people, handwritten notes are more appreciated than emails.

Hopefully, these meetings will give you a good start in discovering opportunities of interest. If you identify a specific job you want to do, then you can begin to identify organizations that need someone like you. If you have not decided, keep exploring different possibilities. The answer might come when you least expect it.

Recommended Actions

Review your thinking about your priorities with regard to where you work next, especially:
1. What is most important to you.
2. The values and culture of where you want to work.
3. Your competencies and preferred role.
4. The contributions you want to make.

Develop a new or revised resume.
1. Have the objective state what you want to do.
2. Show specific competencies, three at the most.
3. Give accomplishments with metrics for each job.
4. Make your Education Section brief and factual.
5. Have the Other section give a broader sense of who you are, your interests and involvements.
6. Prepare to answer potential questions.

Identify and select your references.
1. Explain what you are looking to do and why.
2. Show appreciation for their support.
3. Periodically update them on your progress.

Create your Elevator Pitch.
1. Prepare a brief statement of what you want to do next, your qualifications, and your contributions.
2. If appropriate, ask for suggestions.

Determine the market for your services.
1. Your prior compensation is a good starting point.
2. Use surveys & websites.
3. Contact anyone you think could be helpful.

Identify industries and organizations with products, and/or services where you might want to work.
> 1. Meet with seasoned people you respect to get their thoughts and referrals.
> 2. Explore any areas you think could be interesting.
> 3. Stay open minded and keep at it.

Notes

Notes

Chapter 7 - Your Network

Networking is about connecting with and developing mutually beneficial relationships with people you respect, especially those with similar values to yours. It is the most productive way to get a lead for a job that is right for you. When I was at Heidrick & Struggles, 70% of our placements came from referrals. Chrysalis is a nonprofit in Los Angeles that helps homeless people find jobs. Even at this level, 60% of those who got a job heard about it from someone else. You began networking when you met with people to get their thoughts about their work and opportunities they see. Then you can network with more focus.

List of Contacts

At this phase of your search, you will have to broaden your list of sources to help you find job opportunities. Think of people you know, even slightly, and write down the names of anyone you think might be helpful.

Make several lists, such as:

- **Work**: People with whom you have worked, including bosses, peers, and customers.
- **Strategic**: People in responsible positions in business and service professions. This includes lawyers, business consultants, bankers, and leaders in other fields.
- **Personal**: People whom you like and respect and with whom you have some relationship, including family, friends, and acquaintances as well as those you know through school, college, social, religious affiliation, volunteer organizations, sports and community.

(Source: Harvard Business Review article, *How Leaders Create and Use Networks*)

Setting Priorities

Once you have identified people in all three categories, prioritize your list in a way that makes the most sense to you. If you are still developing your thinking, start with people with whom you would feel most comfortable approaching. They are likely to help you develop your thoughts. Then expand your search to the rest of the people on your list.

One never knows ahead of time where the next job lead will originate. Studies have shown that people get more job leads from acquaintances than from friends. Why? Because friends' networks often overlap and therefore are not as broad as acquaintances'. Therefore, call everyone on your list and those whom they recommend to you. The most productive lead may come from someone at the bottom of your list or who was not on it before you began networking.

George quit his job in major account sales for a consumer products company. He began networking and after a few months was well along in securing another position. Then, out of the blue, he received a call from the CEO of a privately owned company that was starting up a new business in George's specialty. The CEO heard about George from someone in George's network and approached him about taking the sales lead for the new business. This led to George being hired. He is now successfully leading the new venture's sales and has a high level of input into product development. George's network paid off. Yours could too.

When you call people in your network, explain why you are calling and emphasize that you are interested in their perspective and thoughts about opportunities they might see. Then let them know that you would appreciate meeting them whenever they are available. If they prefer not to meet, they may agree to a video (Zoom or other) or phone call. However, in person meetings are by far the most productive.

As your search broadens, you will reach out to people who have similar interests or backgrounds to yours whom you may not know well. In these cases, send the person an e-mail or note referring to your common background and explaining that you are making a career change and would like to get their perspective. Let them know that you will call them. Then do it.

If you do not know anyone in an area of interest and cannot get a referral, you could try going online to identify someone to approach. If that does not work, find a business directory at a library and identify the appropriate role of someone whom you would like to contact. Call the office and ask for the name and address of the person in that role. Then write or email that person explaining that you are exploring opportunities and would appreciate their meeting with you. Follow-up with a phone call.

Some people try to get job leads by going to network gatherings. Most of the people there will also be searching for job leads or are in a service business looking for prospects. You might get some useful information or even a lead by comparing notes with someone with whom you connected and liked. Other types of potentially productive meetings include alumni gatherings, industry conferences, or events with speakers in areas of interest to you. However, networking with people on your lists and others to whom you have been referred will be the most productive.

Meetings

At the beginning of a meeting with a potential source, thank him/her for meeting with you and ask if he/she has any time constraints. Follow with a short summary of your experience and thoughts about what you are looking to do. Then say that you would appreciate getting his/her work experience and thoughts about opportunities in his/her world. Open-ended questions are usually the best way to begin. Be curious, respectful, and appreciative throughout the meeting.

After you learn about the person's experience and perspective, you can ask him/her to tell you more about something that seems particularly interesting to you. Hopefully, the person will recommend people or organizations to contact. If he/she does not, ask if he/she could suggest someone who might be helpful in your search.

Keep on the lookout for something that might be of interest to those whom you are meeting. This could be as simple as giving an overview of what you have learned from your search so far.

Those you met would appreciate receiving a handwritten note or an email thanking them for the time they took with you. In doing this, mention what you thought was most important and helpful. Later, if a referral turns out to be productive, let the person who gave it to you know and thank him/her. This will strengthen your relationship.

Recommended Actions

Identify and make lists of people whom you think could help you find opportunities.
1. **People you know from work**, recently and in the past.
2. **People who have a broader perspective,** such as professionals in service industries and community leaders.
3. **Friends and family** from all aspects of your life.

Prioritize each list in a way that makes sense for you.
1. Include each person's name, phone number, email and organization.
2. Organize yourself and keep good records.

Prepare a short script for your meetings.
1. Review your objectives for your meetings.
2. Prepare a basic script.

Begin your networking by calling potential sources of leads. Be organized and persistent.
1. If you feel uncertain, start with people with whom you feel most comfortable and ask for feedback.
2. Then broaden your networking as you gain experience and confidence.

3. Seek referrals for job leads and sources.
4. Make networking something you do every day.

In your meetings with sources:
1. Let the person know that you appreciate his/her meeting with you and ask if he/she has any time constraints.
2. Give a summary of your situation and thoughts about it.
3. Ask what is happening in his/her world and what opportunities he/she sees.
4. Ask if he/she has any suggestions or referrals.
5. Always follow up your meetings with a note or e-mail thanking him/her.

Actions for continuing to network:
1. Keep records of people you meet.
2. Make weekly plans for all that you are doing.
3. Periodically review what you have learned and make any changes or redirections you think are appropriate.

In addition to using the reminder of this page and the next, consider using the space in the back of the book for your notes.

Notes

Notes

Chapter 8 - Other Search Approaches

In addition to networking, there are other ways to uncover good opportunities. The Internet is an important one. Directly approaching organizations of interest and connecting with search firms can also deliver results. All together these account for one third of the way people get jobs.

Internet

LinkedIn.com is currently the most important portal. Organizations looking to hire someone will often screen LinkedIn profiles and contact those who are qualified for a given opportunity. Most executive search professionals have a premium membership that enables them to search the LinkedIn database in many ways.

To get the most benefit from LinkedIn, put a good deal of thought and time into your Profile and keep it up to date. Your Profile will have more impact if it highlights your competencies and uses active verbs, direct language, and no superlatives. In addition, it should communicate something about your personal interests, breadth of experience, and contributions to your community. Having a professional photo is critical for getting traction with LinkedIn.

LinkedIn has contracts with many corporations that post job openings on LinkedIn. It will sort through the various listings and identify the openings that match your profile. LinkedIn enables you to apply to any listing of interest to you.

LinkedIn also has organized discussion groups on many business and professional areas. Joining one could help you learn, get ideas, and leads.

When applying for a position on LinkedIn or elsewhere, look on LinkedIn to see if you know anyone is with or formerly was at the organization with the opening. If you identify someone, send him/her a message to see if he/she could help with information on the company/role or endorse you to the hiring department or recruiter.

monster.com and **careerbuilder.com** are two websites where someone can post a resume at no cost. They are funded by companies that seek qualified job candidates. Monster.com sorts the job postings and shows people listings that match their interests and background. On Careerbuilder.com, an individual can post his/her resume and search the website by job title and geographic area. Both websites offer other services.

Indeed.com is a robust website that aggregates job listings from many websites. It provides an overview of what is available by job categories and region. If you want to post your resume on the site and have Indeed.com sends you info about new postings.

Indeed.com has reviews of many companies, including postings by former employees who give their thoughts about the company. This could help you predict if the culture of an organization would be a good fit for you. Indeed.com offers additional services.

Glassdoor.com is another website that not only provides information on job opportunities in one's area but also is useful for getting information on compensation and culture. It has pro and con comments about some companies by those who have worked there or may still be there.

Craigslist at **craigslist.itsmycareer.com**. offers many jobs postings and services.

Direct Approach

When answering an ad, a well-done letter expressing your interest in the job can sometimes lead to an interview. If you answer an ad, state your accomplishments and competencies that relate directly to the position. To demonstrate your interest and initiative, say that you will follow up with a phone call. Since your resume contains more about you than is relevant to the job posted, it can distract whoever is reviewing your letter. Therefore, enclose a resume only when one is requested. The odds of your getting an interview are not good, but it can work. I know several people who got jobs at Xerox Corporation from answering newspaper ads.

Approaching individual companies is another option. Many large companies have job postings on their websites and in-house recruiters who keep a file of resumes and access them when conducting a search. Small companies have less staff and structure, but often are on the lookout for people that fit their profile. Doing this is a long shot but sending an unsolicited resume might get traction either at the time it is received or later.

Search Firms

Contingency Search Firms get paid when a company hires one of the people that the firm has brought to them. They specialize in industry and/or job function. They have relationships with their client organizations and understand each organization's employment needs. They are on the lookout for professionals and managers who would fit in with their clients.

If you are a professional or manager, it could be worthwhile sending your resume to contingency search firms that specialize in your field. If one of these firms has called you in the past, call them. If no firm comes to mind, one of your peers might have a suggestion. Otherwise, you could search online for appropriate Contingency Search Firms.

Retained Executive Search Firms are paid a fee to identify, meet, and assist with the recruiting of senior managers, executives, and boards of directors. There are about a half-dozen large, well-established firms and many small, independent ones. Individual search consultants in large and small firms often specialize in industry and sometimes function. The searches conducted by these firms have specific qualifications and experience specifications that limit the number of qualified candidates for any one search.

If you are at a level that would qualify you to be a candidate for an Executive Search Firm, you could identify and connect with professionals in these firms. One of them may have called you in the past. If not, check with your peers for recommendations. Otherwise, call these firms' offices in your area and ask who within the firm specializes in your industry or function. Send that person a cover letter and resume. But keep in mind that the probability of this leading to a job is slim. In the 23 years I was with Heidrick & Struggles, only once was one of my placements someone who had sent me an unsolicited resume.

Large search firms will sometimes keep resumes for use in future searches. Small search firms seldom do, but many are members of the Association of Executive Search and Leadership Consultants (AESC) that keeps resumes for member firms to access. To get in this file, send your resume to **bluesteps.com/content/homepage** expressing your interest in being a candidate or source of candidates for their searches.

By far the most important thing you can do to progress in your working life is to do your job well and develop good relationships with those with whom you work. Consider Elizabeth's experience.

Elizabeth *grew up in Florida and graduated from the University of Florida. At the suggestion of a friend who had joined the Turner organization in Atlanta, she applied for and was accepted into the Turner Temp Program. For six months, she worked at several business units, then joined CNN and began a 15-year career there. She found the Turner organization's culture to be open, collaborative, and innovative.*

Elizabeth's first job was answering viewers' calls and dealing with questions and comments about programs. She learned what viewers liked and did not like. She felt this was a great introduction to CNN's market. After seven months, she became an assistant to a marketing director who had responsibility for promoting CNN's brand and engaging new audiences. In a reorganization, her department became Marketing and Creative Services. Elizabeth's job evolved into reading film scripts, creating advertising for CNN programming, and supporting the firm's editorial partnerships with magazines.

Over the years, Elizabeth progressed to Senior Director of Marketing with responsibility for people in marketing strategy, advertising, and off-channel creative activities. She often travelled to New York City to coordinate various projects. Elizabeth spent so much time in New York City that she asked for and received approval to move there.

Elizabeth had been in New York about a year when she was approached by an executive search consultant for a senior marketing position in a major broadcast organization. The consultant had found Elizabeth through her LinkedIn profile.

At first, Elizabeth was intrigued but declined as she really liked CNN. A couple of weeks later, the consultant called back and told Elizabeth that her name kept coming up. The search consultant asked her to meet with him. Elizabeth was curious and met the consultant.

The position at the other network was attractive. Elizabeth had not been planning to leave CNN. Yet, she never thought she would be a lifer. After the interview with the client and offer, Elizabeth was still undecided. Then the consultant told her that if she was ever going to leave CNN, this was the time. She had options now, but she might not later. Elizabeth decided to make the leap and was soon hired as Senior Director of Marketing with the responsibility for brand strategy and network promotions.

Elizabeth immediately went to work hiring a team of brand managers. She found the culture at this network quite different from CNN's. Many people thought in terms of the good old days when the network was dominant. They operated in silos with little communication between silos.

After a year or so Elizabeth realized that the network was "killing" an unusual number of promotions. This often happened when the news ran over. This was a major concern for Elizabeth, especially when she found out that the value of the promotions being killed came to millions of dollars. When she presented this to senior management, they ordered this stopped.

Two and a half years after Elizabeth joined the network, she received a phone call from the president of a marketing agency whom she knew well. She had used the agency for this network and when she was with CNN. The President approached Elizabeth about joining the agency as Senior Vice President & Group Head of its Entertainment Group, which had major global clients. Elizabeth had a high respect for the executive and the agency. She was interested. This call was followed by a couple of additional calls and then an offer. With the encouragement of her mentor, Elizabeth accepted the offer.

At the marketing agency, Elizabeth is a member of senior management. Clients are major news, media, and digital organizations. She leads a team of creative, production, and accountancy employees who work closely with their clients to develop long-term brand platforms designed to affect culture, address big societal issues, and generate revenue. The agency has won many awards. Elizabeth is happy there.

Elizabeth made two successful transitions, contributed to each organization, and developed strong relationships. Her contributions and relationships have enabled her to be successful in all her roles. She made career changes while in positions of strength and built on her success. Your relationships and contributions should be the basis for your career progress too.

Recommended Actions

Develop and utilize a LinkedIn account.
1. State your current position and/or the position you are pursuing with a title you think would be picked up by search engines.
2. Describe your experience and accomplishments giving metrics but no embellishments.

3. Include a formal photograph of yourself.
4. Begin connecting with LinkedIn's services.

Visit and explore other websites mentioned in this chapter.
1. Explore both monster.com and careerbuilders.com and submit your info for opportunities that look interesting.
2. Check out Indeed.com, Glassdoor.com, and Craigslist.

Answer ads and/or send letters without referrals as appropriate.
1. Search publications that you think are likely to post ads for opportunities of interest.
2. Respond to postings that look right for you.
3. Write to people you want to meet but to whom you have no connection. Try to get meetings.
4. Look for and respond to job posts at websites of organizations of interest.

Contact search firms that you feel are appropriate.
1. Mail a resume to members of appropriate search firms.
2. If you are a senior manager or executive, send your resume to **bluesteps.com** to get visibility with small search firms.

Develop a search plan that includes:
1. Networking as your primary activity.
2. Visiting and posting on LinkedIn and other websites.
3. Going to meetings and appropriate events.
4. Contacting search consultants.
5. Answering ads.
6. Approaching people and organizations of interest where you do not have an introduction.
7. Being available for your personal relationships.
8. Keeping in good physical and mental shape.

Notes

Section III - Interviewing

Your interviews with potential employers are the most important interactions for joining the right organization. To get the most out of them, devote plenty of time and thought preparing for each meeting. In your interviews be thoughtful and professional as you answer questions and describe what you have accomplished. Be sure to get a good sense of the people you meet, their values and the culture of the organization. At the conclusion of your interviews, both you and the hiring manager should have a good understanding of each other. Both of you want to be sure you would relate well to the people in the organization and do a good job once there.

Chapter 9 - Interview Preparation

Since job interviews are the most important step in the process of getting a job that is right for you, it is critical that you put time and thought into preparing for each interview.

Research the Organization

Before an interview find out all you can about the organization and the specific group in which you might work. Most large organizations have an overall culture, but each subset will have its own. Search LinkedIn and other websites for information about the organization. To learn what you can about a specific group, try to talk with someone who once worked there or has dealt with the group.

Prepare Questions

Prior to the day of an interview, prepare a list of questions about the organization to help you get a feel for the job and people, their values, personalities, and thoughts about where they are working. Areas of inquiry are:

1. The job, including responsibilities, challenges, and expected results. How this position relates to others.
2. How the previous person in the job performed and where he/she is now.
3. Something you learned about the company.
4. The interviewer's history with the company and thoughts about it.
5. How an important decision was made and implemented. Was it bottom up or top down? To what extent was there good collaboration?

Creating a list will help prepare you for your interview and demonstrate your preparation and interest in the organization.

Prepare to Answer Questions

Reflect on what you have contributed to the organizations where you have worked and the capabilities you would bring to an organization. Expect that each person who interviews you will have his/her own perspective depending on his/her position in the organization:

- <u>The hiring manager</u> will be interested in how well you would perform the job and work with the team.
- <u>The human resources person</u> will want to know if you have the qualifications specified for the job and if there are any issues that might eliminate you as a candidate.
- <u>Peers</u> will want to know if you will get along well with them as a team member and do your part.
- <u>Others</u> will mostly want to learn about your values, personality, and how they feel about you.

Review your resume and think about how you would respond to questions, such as:

- The reasons and circumstances relating to each of your job changes. Emphasize positives and avoid negatives.
- Your successes. Be clear about your roles and what you accomplished. Quantify your impact when you can.
- Mistakes. Being open and positive about what you did and learned will give you credibility.
- The reasons behind your most important decisions, especially your values, thinking process, and priorities. Keep your answers well focused without much detail.

Prepare yourself mentally for an interviewer to challenge you by asking how you might handle an issue relating to the job for which you are interviewing. If you get a difficult question and need time to think, ask for some clarification of the question. Interviewers are mostly interested in how you address problems and your priorities. They are not looking for a 'right' answer.

If you have had multiple jobs in a short period or have gaps in employment, you should expect questions about these. You could respond with facts and reasons without getting into the details. If they were due to mistakes of yours and you say what you learned from them, you will gain credibility.

Before interviewing, review what you have already learned about the market value of someone with your experience and qualifications. If necessary, update your thinking by checking online and/or talking to someone who is active in the market.

Recommended Actions

Do your homework on the organization before your first interview.
1. Try to talk to someone who has knowledge of the group you would be joining.
2. Go online to the organization's website and others, such as Google, LinkedIn, indeed, and Glass Door.

Develop a list of questions that will enable you to get a good sense of the job and people there. Ask about:
1. The job responsibilities, deliverables, and issues.
2. How the job relates to other positions in the organization.
3. Recent history of the organization and the job.
4. Your interviewers' feelings about working there.

Prepare for questions that you may be asked, such as:
1. Your relevant experience for the job.
2. Reasons for job and career changes.
3. Challenges you have faced and how you handled them.

Update what you have learned about the compensation range for someone with your capabilities and experience.

Notes

Chapter 10 - The Classic Job Interview

Always prepare for each interview, find out what you can about those you will be meeting. When asked a question in an interview, address the question and thought behind it and be true to yourself. Observe the interviewer and ask questions to get a good sense of his/her values and the organization - its culture, operating environment, and what it does for its customers/clients.

Preparation

Before you have your first interview, find out the approximate compensation level the employer has established for the position to save unnecessary effort. If the level is about what you consider your services to be worth, then proceed. If it is significantly less, consider cancelling the interview. If you are unable to find out the compensation level and the job looks interesting, then take the interview.

To find out useful information for your interview, call the organization a day or two before and ask to speak to the administrative assistant of your contact. Then confirm the name, title, and responsibilities of the person you are meeting and others who might be there too. Also, find out the proper dress code and where to park your car. If you feel good about the person to whom you are speaking, consider asking if he/she can think of anything else you might want to know.

Pre-interview

Avoid unnecessary stress by leaving extra time for travel to the organization where you will be interviewed. Once there, observe the people and premises and look at any available literature about the organization. Be courteous and thoughtful to everyone you encounter. When I was at Heidrick & Struggles, my administrative assistant always met interviewees in the waiting room and brought them to my office. After they left, I made a point of asking her what she thought of them and considered what she said as I decided whether to present them to my client. It made a difference if the person was discourteous or off-putting in some way.

Some tips for a successful interview:
1. Project confidence. Be positive. Smile.
2. Shake hands firmly and look the other person in the eye unless the interviewer's culture entails greeting people in a different manner.
3. Be attentive to the interviewer's perspective.
4. When answering a question, listen carefully and think about both the question and what might have prompted it.
5. Show interest in and appreciation for what the interviewer's organization has accomplished.
6. Express personal interest in the interviewer -- his/her role, feelings about what he/she is doing, and thoughts about the organization.

Interview Phases

The <u>first phase</u> of the interview is about first impressions, the interviewer's and yours. At the outset, convey that you are interested in meeting him/her and try to get a good sense of the interviewer.

- Greet the interviewer warmly. Confirm that you have his/her name and title correct and do the same for any others present.

- Look around the interviewer's office to learn as much as you can about him/her. Are there trophies or pictures related to work, family, or personal interests? Be positive in your small talk. You might ask a question or comment on something you see.

- Find out how much time the interviewer has allotted for the interview.

The interviewer controls the <u>second phase</u>. Your goal is to give the interviewer an understanding of what you have accomplished and could contribute to his/her organization. You can find out a lot about the organization and interviewer by observing the interviewer's approach, focus, and questions. Try to:

- Answer the questions asked and address the underlying issues you sense are behind them.
- Determine what interests the interviewer and on what he/she focuses - accomplishments, process, relationships, or something specific.
- When describing accomplishments, provide metrics and be sure to give credit to your team members.

If the interviewer expresses great interest in one part of your background or passes over something that you think is important, ask the interviewer why. You might learn something.

When you think, you have responded to what the interviewer wanted to cover, ask the interviewer if you can pose some questions. If he/she agrees, take the lead and ask your questions. If the interviewer still has a question or two, then ask if you could pose your questions later.

The third phase is your opportunity to lead and find out about the job, the people, the organization, and whatever else on your mind that has not been covered. By referring to your list, you will see an appropriate question and demonstrate that you prepared for the interview. Most interviewers encourage the interviewee to ask questions because the questions reflect a lot about the interviewee.

If you do not have a sense for the compensation level of the position at this point late in the interview, ask what the organization has set for it. If the interviewer responds by asking what you have in mind, say that you are interested in the position and how much the organization values it. If pressed further, say what your research disclosed and/or your previous compensation. If the interviewer does not want to answer your question, let it go.

The fourth phase of the interview is the closure phase. Your goal is to uncover any remaining questions on the interviewer's mind and confirm your interest in the job.

- Ask the interviewer if he/she has any remaining questions. (Experienced interviewers often ask especially sensitive questions at this point.)
- If you feel good about your interview, express your interest in joining his/her team.
- Ask about the next steps. If the answer is vague, ask when you might hear back from the interviewer.
- Thank the interviewer for his/her time and attention.

Post-Interview

Try to leave a good impression.
- Be positive, courteous, and show interest in all the employees you encounter.

- Soon after the interview, send the interviewer a handwritten note thanking him/her, expressing your interest, and referring to something specific. Emails are not as personal but depending on the culture of the group may be appropriate.

I once met with the Chief Financial Officer of a major wine company to do a search for a controller reporting to him. *During the interview, the CFO made the statement that the job was a simple one and that the responsibilities were straightforward. (In preparation for the meeting I had found out that three people had been in the job during the past two years.) I asked why this was. The CFO responded to my question with bluster. He hemmed and hawed but he did not answer my question. This left me feeling uncomfortable about recruiting anyone to work for him. Soon after this, we ended the meeting because I decided not to pick up the search.* If you ever get an uneasy feeling about someone who is interviewing you, pay attention to your gut instincts and act accordingly.

When the interviewee and the interviewer connect in values and style, things can happen very quickly. *I know an experienced Wall*

Street trader who was being considered by a brokerage firm for a position to trade the firm's funds. To prepare for the interview with the head of trading, the candidate wrote on the soles of his shoes— "Fuck" on one and "Goldman" on the other. (Goldman Sachs was the leading competitor.) At the beginning of the interview, he put his shoes up on top of the desk of the head of trading. The head of trading looked at them and said, "You're hired."

To have a successful interview, you must have a good sense of who you are, what you want to do, and the culture and values of where you want to work. Always be true to yourself, present yourself as you are, and develop a good understanding of the people and organization. If you feel good about the people and the organization, then proceed. Otherwise, do not.

Recommended Actions

Prepare for the interview by learning all you can about:
1. The organization and its people.
2. The role of those whom you will be meeting.
3. The compensation level or range.

And:
4. Prepare a list of questions to ask.
5. Prepare answers to questions you may be asked.

Call the office of the interviewer a day or two before the Interview and confirm:
1. The time and place of the interview.
2. The names and titles of those you will meet.
3. The logistics for parking and where to meet.
4. The organization's dress code.

In the interview:
1. Focus on the interviewer's questions.
2. Keep your answers short and factual.
3. Find out what you can about the job, its role, deliverables, challenges, and its history, if any.
4. Get a sense of the peoples' values and culture.
5. Refer to your list and ask about something on it.

6. Find out the compensation level set for the job.
7. Express interest in the job and joining the organization.

After the interview:
1. Ask yourself what you have learned and how you feel about the people, job, and organization?
2. Write or email the interviewer thanking him/her with some specifics about your interest in the job.
3. If you have not heard from the employer after a week, call your contact and ask where your candidacy stands.

Notes

Chapter 11 - Other Interview Situations

When preparing for, participating in, or following up on an interview, keep in mind the classic interview concepts discussed in the last chapter. Although the process is similar, the context of the interview and the objectives can be unique for other types of interviews.

Types of Interviews

Telephone interviews are often used to screen potential candidates prior to inviting them for an in-person interview.
1. Find out who will be conducting the telephone interview.
2. Develop a clear idea of what you want to say about yourself without going into too much detail.
    a. Accomplishments
    b. Competencies
    c. Answers to likely questions
3. Use some version of your elevator pitch tailored to the job opportunity.
4. Keep your answers short and to the point.
5. Ask about the responsibilities and challenges of the job, and express interest in it.

Group interviews are in many ways like one-on-one interviews in terms of preparation and process. Specifics for group interviews:

In the interview:
1. Expect one of the employer's team to lead the discussion.
2. Look at each person more than once.
3. If some of the people have not asked any questions, ask each if he/she has any.
4. Get a sense for the leader and others in the group by observing their demeanor and interactions.

After the interview:
1. Write a letter or send an email to your contact and the most senior person there if he/she was not your contact.
2. If after a week you have not heard from your contact, call him/her and ask where your candidacy stands.

<u>Video interviews</u> are like other interviews but through media and require you to plan how you present yourself.
1. Make sure that the computer is at eye level. (If your computer is at desk level, the viewer will mostly be looking at your chin and up your nose.) A few books placed under the computer helps.
2. Have appropriate background décor. (If you are in a bedroom, keep the beds out of view.)
3. Make sure that the light is on your face coming from the front and is soft. (If it is behind you, your face will be in a shadow.)
4. Have your speech reflect your normal, professional self - simple, direct language with a measured pace and tone.
5. Practice with a friend to make sure you are properly prepared for the session using Zoom Meetings or another system.

<u>Follow-up interviews</u> indicate the organization has continued interest in you. However, the hiring organization may have one or two other candidates who are also under consideration.

If you are invited back to meet other members of the organization, find out each person's role and the relationship that person has to the job for which you are interviewing. These people are most interested in getting a sense of how they would feel about working with you. You will have the same question about them. To find out how well they work together, ask them how the team members interact and the role of the previous person in the job for which you are interviewing.

A meeting with the hiring manager could be the final interview before he/ she decides whether to make you an offer. To prepare for this meeting review your notes to clarify your thinking about:
1. The job and people you met.
2. The opportunities and challenges of the job.
3. The hiring manager's values and operating style.
4. The culture of the organization.

If you sense that this could be the last meeting with the hiring manager before you might receive an offer and if compensation has not been discussed, ask if it would be appropriate to do so. If the answer is "no," ask where your candidacy stands. The hiring manager might need to get feedback from the other people who interviewed you that day. However, if he/she is interested in proceeding with you, he/she will want to get your thoughts as much as you want his/hers.

If you meet the hiring manager's boss, it is likely that the hiring manager has chosen you and wants the boss's blessing. In addition to answering the boss's questions, be sure to show enthusiasm for joining the organizations and have thoughtful reasons why you are interested. Also, you have an opportunity to gain a broader perspective on the organization by asking what his/her priorities are and the opportunities and challenges he/she sees for the organization. If you feel comfortable doing this, do so.

Observations

All interviews, especially follow-up ones, can tell you a lot about the organization and group you might join. The more time and effort the hiring organization takes to vet candidates, especially if they have candidates meet many people there, the better. Organizations with a lengthier hiring process get to know the candidate better. This improves the probability someone hired will do well there.

If you are a final candidate for a position and you have met only the hiring manager and feel that you do not have a good sense for the values and culture of the organization, ask if you could meet some of the people with whom you would be working. Such meetings will help you determine how you would feel about working there. Meeting potential colleagues will also help you start well once you join. Having been involved in your being hired, they will have more interest in seeing you succeed.

Recommended Actions

For each meeting:
1. Do your best to find out the context and format of each meeting.
2. As with any interview, learn as much as you can beforehand about who you will be meeting, the organization and job.
3. Present yourself in the context of the job.
4. Ask questions about the job and team and express interest in the job and joining the team.
5. Follow up appropriately.

Notes

Section IV
Closure and New Beginning

When the interviewing has gone well and is almost over, it is important that compensation, benefits, and related subjects have been discussed. This can avoid issues later. Also, references should be prepared for a call from someone with the hiring organization.

To get closure on an opportunity, be alert and flexible with a positive outlook. In some cases, negotiations are appropriate. In others, they are not. The same is true about getting an offer or not. Whatever the results, view it as the best outcome for you, which it most likely is. Keep in mind that your top priority is to get a job in a place where you feel good about what you would be doing and the values, culture, and mission of the people there.

After accepting an offer and starting with your new employer, work hard to take over your responsibilities promptly and make an extra effort to develop good relationships with your boss and colleagues.

Chapter 12 - Compensations & References

If the interviews have gone well and there is a good chance that an offer will be extended, important aspects of the compensation should be addressed before an offer is made. Also, prior to the organization extending an offer, someone will call references. They should be prepared for that call.

Compensation

Organizations' approach to compensation and benefits varies quite a bit. Large organizations are more structured than small ones. Early stage and entrepreneurial organizations are often flexible and have little structure. There are many aspects of compensation beyond salary and bonus including starting date, healthcare, pension, retirement benefits, and relocation reimbursement. Some positions include a performance-based bonus, stock options, or grants to senior people and critical specialists.

If your interviewing has progressed well and you are being considered for an offer, you will likely discuss compensation and other important considerations. Usually, the hiring manager will bring the subject up, but not always. He/she may think that your preliminary discussions covered these topics. If the manager does not mention this, you should. Using a conditional voice, ask if an offer were made, what would be the range.

The hiring manager may ask you what you have in mind. It is not wise to give a specific number. However, you might divulge your most recent compensation and/or what your research has disclosed.

Some considerations that you may want to discuss are:
- Benefits & policies, such as employee education reimbursement, vacation, and retirement.

- Relocation, either immediately or later, including:
    a. Reimbursement coverage, if available.
    b. Issues with your spouse's employment.
    c. Issues with children in school.
- Personal commitments that may require time off, adjusted hours, or something else.

Once you have a sense of what the offer might include, you can then decide how you will respond. If you have a question, this is the time to bring it up. For instance, you may have to leave your current employer with significant unvested funds in a retirement account or an unpaid bonus you earned.

Organizations have often dealt with compensation issues by offering the new employee a hiring bonus to keep the job offer in the range of established policies. Even organizations with strict compensation guidelines usually do not have restrictions on hiring bonuses. Reimbursement for unusual relocation expenses could also be an important consideration as can an unusual circumstance. Hiring bonuses can deal with these.

You always want to come across as the most interested in contributing to your employer. Compensation is secondary. If you emphasize it, some senior person may think that you are too focused on compensation and not approve of your being hired.

References

To maintain control, give your references' contact information to a potential employer only when someone from the employer's organization is about to call them. Then you can prepare your references each time they might receive a call.

If you think you are near the final stage, you could inquire if the hiring manager plans to call your references. The answer can tell you a lot about where your candidacy stands. If you learn that the hiring organization is not at the point of calling them, then try to find out why not. Your candidacy may not be as far along the process as you think. There could be other candidates being considered. There may be an internal issue. The organization may have already referenced you.

Someone calling references may call others besides the ones you provided. If your search is confidential, you could ask that no one at your employer be called other than the names you have given.

Recommended Actions

Enter a compensation discussion in depth only if there is a good chance that the offer will be extended.
1. Use the hiring organization's compensation structure as the framework.
2. Surface special issues and/or questions you have.

Give out your references.
1. Give references' information to potential employers late in the process.
2. Prepare your references for a call from someone in the organization.
3. If the hiring organization does not want to call your references, try to find out why not.

Notes

Chapter 13 - Getting an Offer or Not

Going through a long process and not knowing the outcome is difficult, especially when there is a possibility that all your effort could result in not getting an offer. In any case, be prepared for any eventuality and take whatever comes with equanimity and a feeling that it is for the best, which it usually is.

Good offer

Once you decide to accept the offer, call your new boss, enthusiastically accept the offer, and discuss a starting date. In doing so, give yourself a week or so off to decompress from the stress you and your loved ones have been feeling. Also, promptly send a letter to make your acceptance official.

Thank your references for their support and let them know about your good fortune. You could ask if they were called and if there was anything they would like to share. Thank them for their help.

During your search, you met many people and formed good relationships with some of them. Strengthen those relationships by contacting them, letting them know your good news and thanking them for their support.

Marginal Offer

If you receive an offer that is below what you think your services are worth, let the hiring manager know your enthusiasm about the job but that you have reservations about the level of the offer.

A few years ago, the son of a friend of mine received an offer from an advertising agency that he felt was too low. *He told the hiring manager that he was interested in the agency but felt that his services were worth more than the offer. After some discussion, the hiring manager said he would talk to his partners. They agreed to increase the offer by $10,000, and he accepted it.* He later learned that they wanted to see how aggressive he was and were pleased to see that he pushed back. Note that in a tactful way, he told them that he thought that his services were worth more than they offered. He never said that he would not accept the offer but simply let the hiring manager know his feelings. If you decide to push back on an offer that you think is not enough, consider following this approach.

A hiring bonus is another way to address a low offer. Other possibilities might be the promise of a promotion or a salary review within a year. However, if you accept an offer based on these commitments and the organization fails to honor them, you will have a problem.

Unacceptable Offer

If the offer is unacceptable, then somewhere earlier in the negotiations the difference in expectations was not understood by the two parties. If this happens to you, you could first say something positive about the organization and your interest in joining it. Then say that you think your services are worth much more than the offer, and you wonder if something can be worked out. You could ask on what the compensation was based, a formal system or some other way. Then you might compare this with what your research showed.

If the offer is increased only slightly or some other issue is not resolved and you do not accept the offer, let the people in the organization know that you regard them highly. You might say that if their thinking changes or another position at a higher-level opening, you would appreciate being considered.

No Offer

If you are told that you are not going to receive an offer, you would come across as a professional by thanking whoever gave you this information. Let him/her know that you are disappointed but appreciate that you were considered.

Let your references know that the situation did not work out for you and ask if they were called. If they were, try to find out what questions were posed and anything that could give an insight into why you did not get an offer. This could help you make sure that there are no issues with your references or something else.

Undoubtedly, you are disappointed. However, when an initial opportunity does not work out, another opportunity could materialize. In any case, consider your experience useful. It broadened your perspective, gave you insights into your area of interest, grew your network, and provided interviewing practice.

Stay positive about your ongoing adventure and the new people you meet. *After I left Xerox and was looking for a job, I got to know the founder of an early-stage company, and we discussed my becoming President. After several meetings with the founder and board members, I joined on a trial basis. I was there two months when the founder told me that it was not going to work out. I departed with mixed feelings and resumed my search.*

Not long after that I was approached by Dr. Schlosser at Heidrick & Struggles for the top marketing position for one of his clients. It looked interesting. Dr. Schlosser interviewed me and recommended me to his client. The client declined to interview me. (He thought that I was too well educated!) Then, to my surprise, Dr. Schlosser asked me if I would be interested in joining his firm. I was. We began a process in which I met many partners of the firm, and they checked my references. Then they made me an offer. I accepted. For me, a rejection by one company turned into a great job with another and put me on a career path I have been on ever since.

If you find yourself in a situation where you have no immediate opportunities, do not despair, keep at it. Be optimistic and initiative-taking. A break may happen when you least expect it.

Recommended Actions

If you receive a good offer:
1. Call your new boss, accept the offer and work out a start date, giving yourself time to decompress.
2. Send a letter accepting the offer.
3. Thank you for your references for their support.
4. Contact all those who helped in your search.
    a. Share your news and thank them.
    b. Let the ones you most respect know that you want to stay in touch
5. Take a short vacation.

If you receive a marginal offer:
1. Let the hiring manager know:
    a. You would like to join the team.
    b. You think that your services are worth more than the offer.
    c. Possibly, share your research on comp.
2. Ask if some adjustment could be made to the offer.
3. Try to maintain a positive dialogue and be flexible. (In the end, you may accept the offer.)

If you receive an unacceptable offer:
1. Let the hiring manager know your feelings and explain your thoughts about the offer.
2. Ask if the offer might be increased to what you think is an appropriate level.
3. If not, politely decline the offer.

If you do not receive an offer:
1. Let the hiring manager know that you appreciated the time they devoted to you and wish them well.
2. Consider the process you went through.
    a. What you learned about yourself.
    b. The experience you gained.
    c. How you broadened your network.
3. Call your reference and update them.
    a. If they were called, find out the questions asked and if there were any issues.
    b. Be appreciative of their support.

4. Reactivate your job search.
    a. Revise your search plan as appropriate.
    b. Resume networking and other means of getting leads.
    c. Be positive with friends and loved ones.
5. Maintain an optimistic outlook and keep in mind that an opportunity can materialize at any time.

Notes

Chapter 14 - Joining the New Organization

After you have taken some time off to decompress, focus on getting a good start at your new job. The more you find out ahead of time about the current issues, challenges, and people with whom you will be working, the better prepared you can be. You will have already learned something about these while you were interviewing but not at the level of detail you will need once you are there. After you start, you will be expected to take over your responsibilities promptly, and you will want to develop good relationships with your boss, colleagues, and hopefully, a mentor.

New Boss

Before starting, set up a meeting with your new boss to learn more about the organization's current challenges and what he/she views as your top priorities. Invite him/her for lunch at a nearby restaurant so the two of you have a discussion without being distracted. Your new boss would appreciate your initiative.

While meeting with your new boss, find out more about his/her priorities and concerns. Let your boss know that you will do whatever he/she thinks needs to be done. Also, ask for suggestions about working with people with whom you will have the most contact, their roles, operating styles, and personalities. Treat what your new boss says about your colleagues in confidence to avoid any problems with them later. Once you have talked with your new boss, begin to prepare yourself for your new responsibilities.

Respect and Extra Effort

From your first day at your new job, be humble and show respect for those you meet. Do not project pride about where you worked before. Your boss has probably told your peers what a great hire he/she made. This could cause some resentment toward you. They may ask you about your experiences elsewhere, but they really do not care. The less you say, the better.

You will be establishing your reputation during the first few months on the job. Since you will have a great deal to learn, put in long hours to accelerate coming up to speed and working with your peers. At first, your peers will understand that there is a lot you do not know, but soon they will expect you to take on your full responsibilities.

Good Relationships

Your most important relationship is with your boss. He/she will have the most impact on your success at your new organization. Observing your boss's actions and communication style will enable you to learn how your boss thinks and deals with others. This will help you communicate with him/her and anticipate his/her reactions. If you have not already done so, ask what he/she thinks are your top priorities. Your boss's answer could be different than what you expect.

Make an extra effort to get to know and develop a good relationship with everyone with whom you work. Meet one-on-one to learn each's priorities, how he/she deals with issues, and what he/she might want or need from you. This will help you understand and work well with your colleagues and give you a sense of who you can expect to be helpful and who will be less likely to be.

Those who have a mentor in an organization have a much better chance of progressing. A good mentor is someone with a broad perspective, is at a level in the organization where he/she understands the nuances of the organization's opportunities and politics and is someone with whom you feel rapport. If you identify a prospective mentor, try to develop a relationship with him/her by asking a question about some deeper issue of the organization, such as how he/she sees it evolving over the next few years. This could lead to a mentoring relationship. It might not, but it is worth trying.

Learning through Experience

When you join an organization, have the attitude that you will be there at least a few years and hopefully many more. With a long-term perspective, you will be better able to concentrate on what is most important.

There is a common pattern when someone takes on a new job in a new organization. At first the person learns about the people, the issues, and the opportunities. Next, the person initiates actions to improve the performance of his/her area of responsibility. Once implemented, it takes a while for the results to be evident. Only after time can someone observe what he/she has accomplished and learn from it. This cycle of action and results is a great way to develop good judgement and capabilities. Those who leave before seeing and observing the results of their actions do not benefit from the insights this provides.

At Xerox during its years of explosive growth, some people were promoted before learning the results from changes they implemented. This put them in positions significantly over their heads. They may have experienced great results in their prior job and looked good, but in fact, their success was the result of the momentum of the business and/or actions initiated by their predecessor. They had not contributed much nor matured enough to be successful in a more senior role and suffered the consequences.

The lesson from this is to do your best and stay long enough to learn from the results of actions you implemented. Build your career on your hard work, shared values, relationships, and contributions. In the long run, you will learn, develop, and accomplish more.

Recommended Actions

Make an extra effort to prepare for the new job.
1. Meet with your new boss, away from the office for lunch.
   a. Find out about the issues and opportunities on his/her mind.
   b. Get his/her thoughts about your priorities.

  c. Learn what you can about the people with whom you will be working.
 2. Research about the company and industry.
  a. Talk to knowledgeable people who might give you good insights.
  b. Go online to learn what you can about the organization and people there.
  c. Conduct research about competition and industry.

Start well.
 1. Be humble and respectful, and mostly ask questions.
 2. Work hard to take over your responsibilities promptly.
 3. Learn how your boss thinks and develop a good relationship with him/her.
 4. Get to know and develop good relationships with your fellow employees.
 5. Develop a relationship with a mentor.

Plan to work there long enough to see the results of your actions and develop meaningful relationships with those you respect.

Notes

Notes

Epilogue

Success at any endeavor comes from being in the moment and concentrating on what one is doing. Goals are important. But thinking about goals rather than the task at hand distracts and often leads to poor results and missed goals.

The process of understanding yourself, preparing for your search, interviewing, getting hired, and especially working for your new employer, has many parallels with Olympic Sailing. Olympians spend years practicing and developing their abilities. They want to win a medal, but they must focus on what they are doing at the moment to do so.

In the 1992 Olympics in Barcelona, there was a woman sailing one of the single-handed boats. She was an excellent sailor and had prepared well for the Olympics. However, in the first race, she was over the starting line just before the official starting signal and was disqualified.

The next day, when she was leaving the dock to go to the racing area, she turned and asked, "What's the word?" A trainer answered, "Gold Medal!" In that race too, she was over the starting line early and disqualified. This left her with no points after two races with five to go and in a terrible position. Thinking that she was out of the running for a medal, she decided just to sail her best and enjoy herself for the rest of the regatta. She did very well in the remaining five races, and to her surprise, won a Bronze Medal.

Like the Olympics, it is always best to be in the moment and focus on what one is doing and not some future goal. Consider the following mottos:

The Olympic motto:
> "The most important thing
> In the Olympic Games is
> not to win but to take part.
> Just as the most important
> thing in life is not
> the triumph but the struggle."

Work motto:
> "The most important things in work
> are not money, power, and position.
> Just as in life, they are values,
> relationships, and contributions."

It is unusual that someone finds the right work and right organization at the beginning of his/her career. I hope this book helps you accelerate your discovery of who you are, especially your values, competencies, and preferred role, and you find work in organizations where you feel good about the people, their values and culture, and your contribution there.

About the Author

For more than two decades, Michael Schoettle worked with and placed executives in client organizations as a Partner of Heidrick & Struggles, a leading global executive search firm. He then created and co-managed a course and career coaching program for Executive MBAs at Loyola Marymount University in Los Angeles. In addition, he volunteered for five years at the non-profit Chrysalis, teaching "Job Prep" to felons recently out of prison. Earlier in his career, he worked in sales and marketing for five different business units of Xerox Corporation.

His experiences taught him how people get jobs and the importance of being qualified for the job and relating well to the people and culture of the organization.

He grew up in the Philadelphia area and spent summers on the New Jersey Shore. He learned to sail and race competitively at an early age. In 1952, he crewed on a 5.5 Meter that won its class in the Helsinki Olympics. He stayed involved in Olympic Sailing over the next 40 years, including leading the United States Olympic Sailing Team in Barcelona that won medals in nine out of ten events.

Schoettle has a B.A. from Yale University and an MBA from Harvard University and was a U.S. Naval Officer for three years. He is married with two grown sons.

Bibliography

Bee, Helen L., <u>The Journey of Adulthood</u>, 1996 Prentice Hall, Inc.

Ben–Shahar Tal, <u>Happier: Learn the Secrets of Daily Joy and Lasting Fulfillment</u>, 2007 Mc Graw Hill

Bolles, Richard N., <u>What Color is Your Parachute</u>, 1970, 2017 Ten Speed Press

Bryant, Andrew and Kazan, Ana, <u>Self-Leadership</u> 2013 McGraw Hill

Carnegie, Dale, <u>How to Win Friends and Influence People</u>, 1968 Simon & Schuster, Inc.

Christensen, Clayton, *How Will You Measure Your Life?* 2010 Harvard Business Review

Cloud, Henry D., <u>Integrity</u>, 2006 Harper Collins Publishers

Covey, Stephen R., <u>Seven Habits of Highly Effective People,</u> 1989, 2014 Simon & Schuster, Inc.

Deemer, Candy and Fredericks, Nancy, <u>Dancing on the Glass Ceiling</u>, 2002 McGraw Hill

Drucker, Peter, *Managing Oneself,* 1999 Harvard Business Review

Drucker, Peter, <u>The Essential Drucker</u>, 2005 Collins Business Essentials

Erickson, Erik H., <u>The Life Cycle Completed</u>, 1983 WW Norton & Company Inc.

Faculty, Harvard Business School, <u>Shaping Your Career</u>, 2008 Harvard Business School Publishing Corporation

Friedman, Howard S. and Martin, Leslie R., <u>The Longevity Project</u> 2011 Hudson Street Press

Fromm, Eric, <u>The Art of Loving</u> 1956 Harper & Rowe. Inc.

Gabarro, John J. and Kotter, John P., <u>Managing Your Boss</u> 1993 Harvard Business Review

George, Bill, <u>True North</u>, 2007 Jossey-Bass

Goldsmith, Marshall and Reiter, Mark, <u>What Got You Here</u>

<u>Won't Get You There</u>, 2007 Hyperion Publishers Harvard Business Review
Ibarra, Herminia, *How Leaders Create and Use Networks*, 2007 Harvard Business Review
Kroger, John, <u>Convictions</u>, 2008 Farrar, Straus and Giroux
Kraemer Jr., <u>From Values to Action</u> 2001 Jossey-Bass
Kraemer Jr., <u>Your 168</u> 2020 john Wiley & Sons, Inc
Levinson, Daniel J., <u>The Seasons of a Man's Life</u>, 1978 Ballantine Books
Levinson, Daniel J., <u>The Seasons of a Woman's Life</u>, 1997 Ballantine Books
Lone, Nicholas, <u>The Pathfinder</u>, 2012 Touchstone Books
Lowney, Chris, <u>Heroic Leadership</u>, 2003 Loyola Press
Lowney, Chris, <u>Heroic Living</u>, 2009 Loyola Press
Myers-Briggs, MBTI Basics, **www.myersbriggs.org/-mbti-personality-type/mbti-basics**
Strength-Finder, **www.gallupstrengthscenter.com**
Tett, Gillian, <u>The Silo Effect</u>, 2015 Simon & Schuster
Thaler, Richard, <u>Misbehaving</u>, 2017 W. W. Norton & Company
Useem, Michael, <u>The Leadership Moment</u>, 1998 Random House
Vaillant, George F., <u>Adaptation to Life</u>, 1977 Little Brown & Company
Vaillant, George F., <u>Aging Well</u>, 2002 Little Brown & Company
White, William J., <u>From Day One</u>, 2006 Prentice Hall
Williams, Walter F., <u>Up from the Projects</u>, 2010 Hoover Institution Press
Williams, Ashley, <u>Time Smart</u>, 2020 Harvard Business School Press

Notes

Notes

Notes

Notes

Notes

Made in United States
North Haven, CT
18 May 2023